SONGS OF HOPE

Songs of Hope

By

Grace Noll Crowell

HARPER & BROTHERS PUBLISHERS

NEW YORK *and* LONDON

This book is complete and unabridged
in contents, and is manufactured in strict
conformity with Government regulations
for saving paper.

Foreword

My friend, if the lamp of Hope
Has burned low in your heart,
Let me share with you the lifted flame
That Life has given me.

¶For permission to reprint the poems in this book credit is due the following publications:

The Christian Herald

The Methodist Episcopal Church Publications (North and South)

Good Housekeeping

Unity Publications

Versemaker

International Journal of Religious Education

CONTENTS

SONGS OF HOPE

*

SONGS OF HOPE

This Brave New World

DEWEY-EYED and shining-faced the morning
    Is starting on its journey of today,
Its old wounds healed and seemingly forgotten,
Its old scars wiped away.

This brave new world! How staunchly it arises
From out the darkened covers of the night;
How valiantly it girds itself to enter
The splendid ways of light!

So would I shake the darkness from my eyelids,
So would I don my garments with the dawn,
The old wounds healed, the old scars unremem-
    bered,
And thus I would move on

Into the waiting ways of light and splendor,
My heart's bright banner lifted and unfurled,
That I may be a valiant marching comrade
To this, the brave new world.

Hope

THIS would I hold more precious than fine
   gold,
  This would I keep although all else be lost:
Hope in the heart, that precious, priceless thing,
Hope at any cost.

And God, if its fine luster should be dimmed,
If seemingly through grief it may be spent,
Help me to wait without too much despair,
Too great astonishment.

Let me be patient when my spirit lacks
Its high exuberance, its shining wealth ;
Hope is a matter, often, God, I know
Of strength, of health.

Help me to wait until my strength returns,
Help me to climb each difficult high slope,
Always within my heart some golden gleam,
Some quenchless spark of hope.

The Insistent Power

IN the beginning God . . . " and in the end,
  And in the in-between, forever He
  Is the insistent power, the constant friend,
The steadfast hope of all eternity.
He is life's bread and wine, He is the truth,
He is the ageless, quenchless fire of youth:
Inalienable from birth and life and death,
Inseparable from any roads men go,
Nearer than hands and feet, closer than breath,
The living force beneath all things that grow,
And from above, the strange impelling might
That draws mankind from darkness into light.

The Common Tasks

THE common tasks are beautiful if we
Have eyes to see their shining ministry.
The plowman with his share deep in the
loam,
The carpenter whose skilled hands build a home,
The gardener working with reluctant sod,
Faithful to his partnership with God—
These are the artisans of life, and oh,
A woman with her eyes and cheeks aglow,
Watching a kettle, tending a scarlet flame,
Guarding a little child—there is no name
For these great ministries, and eyes are dull
That do not see that they are beautiful,
That do not see within the common tasks
The simple answer to the thing God asks
Of any child, a pride within His breast:
That at our given work we do our best.

God's Promises

OUT of an olden golden book I take
　　Bright words and weave them into a lus-
　　　trous thing:
A bow of promise for my own heart's sake,
A glory for my spirit's comforting.
And when the day is dark I set it there
Where I can see its colors on the air,
Its fabric spun of God's own precious words,
His everlasting covenant to man:
It pierces through the darkest cloud; it girds
The whole of earth and heaven in its span:
These promises that I have set apart
Into a bow of comfort for my heart.

The Golden Hills

ONCE in a dark and troubled time
    When I saw no road ahead,
    A wise and a kindly counselor
Sat by my side and said:
"Each morning I drive down a valley road
To get to my work, and I
Can often see nothing at all for the fog
That blots out the earth and sky;
But I say to myself, 'I shall drive ahead,
Carefully, without sight.
For I know I shall come onto higher ground
Where the hills are gold with light.'
And I just keep on . . ."
Oh, wise kind words
That fell on my heart that day,
Nothing can blot them from my mind,
Nothing can take them away,
And now when a thick fog shuts me in
To choke me and blind my eyes,
I am so glad for the hills ahead,
For the friend who was kind and wise!

Tomorrow's Bridge

TOMORROW'S bridge as I look ahead
　　Is a rickety thing to view:
　　Its piers are crumbled, its rails are down,
Its floor would let me through.

The chasm it spans is dark and deep,
And the waters foam and fret;
I have crossed that bridge a thousand times
Though I never have reached it yet.

It has crashed beneath me to let me through,
Although it is miles away;
But strange, the bridges that I have crossed
Have all been safe today.

Perhaps I shall find when I reach that one
That lies in the distant blue,
Some hand may have mended its rickety floor
And its piers may be strong and new.

And I can pass over, light-hearted, free,
As a bird on the buoyant air—
Forgive me, God, for my fearful heart,
My anxious and foolish care.

Spring Freshet

I LIKE the look of snow when it is melting
And sending its clear rivulets toward the sea;
I like the sweep of dry grasses bending
Beneath those bright feet, suddenly set free.

I have seen small green leaves under water
That snow had hidden through the winter hours,
Fresher and greener and sweeter than the leafing
That springs to life after the April showers:

A little clover leaf washed clean by waiting,
Eager for life again at the hint of spring!
I reach my fingers into the icy water
To touch that tender, tremulous, wistful thing,

Knowing a kinship with it, deep and abiding,
I, too, have waited until the winter passed,
And I lift my head after a strange chastisement
To the bright air again, the sun at last!

A Church Spire at Sunset

ABOVE the city street a church's spire
   Is climbing its bright ladder to the sky.
   The steeple's slates glow red, its tip is fire,
A single burning finger there, and high
Above that peak a flying white dove swings,
A scarlet light upon its lifted wings.

These are God's emblems, and they call to men
Above the darkening shadows of the street,
Beckoning to them, bidding them hope again,
Bidding them stay a moment their swift feet,
Calling to them to lift their eyes, and there,
Seeing that pointing finger, breathe a prayer.
And the white bird flying heavenward bids them
   cease
The clamor of their hearts and find His peace.

The Light

I KNOW that Jesus lived, and that He died;
And that He rose again, and this to me
Is proof of my own immortality.
There is an empty tomb and by its side
Stands One so radiantly clean and white
That men through all the centuries can see
Beyond the closed doors of eternity,
A Light:

A luminous, clear Light that will not die,
An emanation from the living Christ.
His certain resurrection has sufficed
To blot away all doubt and fear, and I
Who love life so will find there are no bars
To keep my soul from climbing the bright air,
Drawn by that high impelling radiance there
Beyond the stars.

"*They that Wait upon the Lord*"
(ISAIAH XL, 31)

O WEARY one, lay hold on God and claim
This glorious promise, prove its depth and
length,
And let it warm your being like a flame:
Who waits on God, he shall renew his strength.
Your weariness shall pass forevermore;
You shall forget your sorrow and your tears,
You shall be young again—God will restore
The years to you, the seeming wasted years.

You shall mount up as eagles, you shall fly
On strong swift pinions through the dazzling noon,
Or cleave the night on wings to reach the sky,
One with the racing wind, the stars, the moon.
And you shall run and not be weary, Heart,
The golden hills shall fall beneath your feet,
The journey's ending will be as the start,
So fresh you will be, and the way so sweet.
But more than lifting wings, or strength to run,
Will be the joy, after the old restraint:
To walk unburdened, free beneath the sun,
The long bright miles before you, and not faint.

I Shall Be Glad

IF I can put new hope within the heart
  Of one who has lost hope,
  If I can help a brother up
Some difficult long slope
That seems too steep for tired feet to go,
If I can help him climb
Into the light upon the hill's far crest,
I shall begrudge no time
Or strength that I can spend, for well I know
How great may be his need.
If I can help through any darkened hour,
I shall be glad indeed.

For I recall how often I have been
Distressed, distraught, dismayed,
And hands have reached to help, and voices called
That kept me unafraid.
If I can share this help that I have had,
God knows I shall be glad.

"This Same Jesus"

TODAY on the road I met Him:
The very same Jesus who trod
The old, old lanes and the highways
On His beautiful errands for God.

I was troubled and heart-sick and weary
With a load too heavy to bear;
I cried aloud in my weakness
And suddenly He was there,

His gentle hand on my shoulder
Was lifting the burden from me,
And He dried my tears, and I knew Him,
It was Jesus of Galilee:

No different at all from the Master
On the Jericho road that day;
No different at all from the Saviour
Along the Samaria way,

And I am so glad that I met Him!
I knelt and I called out His name,
And I am so grateful I found Him
Unchanged and forever the same.

"The Peaceable Fruit"

(Now no chastening for the present seemeth good; but grievous; nevertheless, afterwards it yieldeth the peaceable fruit of righteousness. HEB. XII, 11)

AFTER the storm there will remain
The brightest fruit on the bough:
The peaceable fruit for your hands to pluck,
Whatever your sorrow now,
Whatever your suffering, O my friend,
Whatever the load you bear,
After the storm the golden fruit
Of the land will be waiting there.

Lift up your hands, make straight the paths,
Though dark the way may seem,
Ahead are the orchards bright in the sun
Where the golden apples gleam.
Let no bitterness trouble your heart,
For after the night is past,
The gold and the scarlet, rain-washed fruit
Of peace will be yours at last.

"Into a Mountain Apart"

WHENEVER the Master could, He stole away
From the great throngs to seek some quiet place
Where He could be alone, where He could pray,
Where God could come to meet Him face to face.
Strange strength is ever born of solitude;
The heart today grows weary of its care
And over-burdened . . . God, it would be good
To seek a mountain side and find Thee there.

Christ stole away at evening to the hills.
So should we go, the press of the day's work done,
To seek some quiet place where the last light spills
The radiant splendor of the setting sun,
And kneel to pray. How often we have lost
The way to solitude, and at such cost!

Sheep Pastures

OUT of the noise and clamor of the town
       I have come down
         To this green pasture land where sheep
Graze in the golden light,
Where shadows creep
As deliberately as they across the grass.
The slow hours pass,
And I am one with the rhythm and the rhyme
Of this still land, this quiet time;
Even my hurrying heart has stayed its pace
Within this quiet place.

Time is nothing here—the sun, the moon,
Come neither late nor soon;
There is no change in the ways of sheep.
They have kept
Step with the ages, hurrying not at all,
And no relentless call
Bids them keep
Appointment with the hours. If I could stay
Day after day
Here in this clean green land, perhaps I, too,
Could be more true

To the movement of the years; could march with
    time
Until the far sublime
Music of the spheres
Would reach my ears,
And I could keep the tempo my life through
That sheep and shepherds do.

In Many Tongues

HE WHO has suffered much speaks many
       tongues.
   He can be understood, he understands
The language of the countless ones who reach
For sympathy with weak imploring hands;
To each in his own tongue he has the words
That bring the quick relief of tears; he speaks
And suddenly old heavy burdens lift,
And there is hope again for him who seeks.

O you who have grown weary of your load,
Shoulder it bravely again a little while.
There will be those who may require of you
Help to go some first bewildering mile
With grief or pain. God will have need of you
As His interpreter that you may tell
Them of the hope ahead, of the healing years,
And of His love. Oh, learn the language well!

Shut-In

I WAKED to a day of darkness and cold rain,
   I said, "Would that the hours were past and the
      day gone."
The wet boughs in the wild wind lashed the pane,
The flowers were sodden splotches upon the lawn.
"Would that the night were here and the hours
      through!"
Restless, my heart cried out, and then there came
A sudden shaft of sun and a stain of blue,
Catching the curtained darkness like a flame.

And there was firelight dancing upon the hearth;
There was a small book weighted with golden lore;
A song rode in on the wind-waves of the earth;
A neighbor breasted the storm to reach my door.
A beloved voice came to me over the wire,
And there was a letter from many a mile away.
Shut-in? My heart was ashamed of its desire;
It would have missed so much had it missed today.

Tulip Bulbs

HANDLE them carefully, gardener! these brown husks
  Have banked their fires, but any moment may
Burst into flame. They hold the dawns and dusks
And the gold noons of every gorgeous day;
They are heavy with age, yet youth will rend them apart,
And color will tear its bright way through their heart.

A breathless interim they now are stilled,
But, gardener, you are dealing with mystery;
These globes encircle magic and are filled
With the wonder of things that were and that are to be.
Slip them quickly under the broken sod,
Lest you, too soon, come face to face with God.

The Glory Way

NOW that the Christ is risen,
Now with the darkness gone,
The road lies out before us,
Upward, and on and on.

There are His sandal footprints,
There is His form ahead,
Straight and strong and compelling,
The Christ that they left as dead.

Nothing can dim His glory,
Nothing can stay His feet,
And countless are they who follow
Him down each lane and street;

And I would be one among them,
Along the Glory Way;
I would arise and follow
The risen Christ today.

I Prayed Today

IN my quiet room I talked with my Friend today;
  I opened my heart to Him with its weight of
    care.
I spoke of the burdens I carried along the way;
I sought His help as I knelt at His feet in prayer.
I told Him my griefs, forgetting He knew them all;
I prayed for my own, forgetting that He could see
Within their hearts each need, though great or
    small,
Each unsolved problem and dark perplexity.

In my quiet room I talked with the Friend I love,
As He engineered His planets, His stars, His suns;
My little world was what I was dreaming of,
My little day, and my own near precious ones.
And He with His hands on the universe, His eyes
Upon endless space and the sweep of eternity,
Bent above me, listening to my cries,
And, forgetting my faults and failures, answered me.

A Song for Comfort

THE things that are too hard to bear
God does not bid me bear.
I never yet have walked alone
Through dark hours of despair,
And always He has kept His word:
The promised strength was there.

And so today, my heart, be still,
He knows that you are torn,
He also knows that even this
Great sorrow can be borne.
His voice still speaks across the years:
"Blessed are they that mourn."

The grief that is too hard to bear
We need not bear, or fear.
Be comforted, remembering
That One who cares is near,
And He will hold us by the hand
Until the dark skies clear.

I Sheltered Many a Care

I SHELTERED many a heavy care
 And hugged them to my bosom,
 I held them close and guarded them
For fear that I should lose them.
One day I sat beside the road
All spent and worn and sighing,
Too tired to listen to the birds,
Or mark the white clouds flying.

Then suddenly, a shining note
Like silver dropped from heaven,
Pierced my ears; the cooling shade
Offered its wayside leaven.
The swaying grasses bent to touch
My fevered cheek, and blessed me;
A wild flower reached its gentle hand
And lovingly caressed me.

The morning dew was like a drink
Of water for my thirsting;
I saw a lark lift from the grass,
His gold throat swelled to bursting.

I rose to take my cares again,
And carefully to bind them
About my heart—but they were gone.
I searched, but could not find them.

Thorns

SHARP were the thorns on my Saviour's brow,
    Forked and crimson-stained,
    .And till the last sharp breath was drawn,
They remained.

Out of great suffering one cried
Thrice to be rid of a thorn,
But from that long unanswered prayer,
Strength was born.

Who am I to be bitter now
Over a bitter thing:
I who am neither evangelist,
Nor a king?

Let it depart from me, O God,
Lighten my path, my days,
But may Thy grace, Thy strength be mine,
If it stays.

Quiet Things

THESE I have loved with passion, loved
    them long:
    The house that stands when the building
    hammers cease,
After wild syncopation, a sane song,
A tree that straightens after the wind's release,
The cool green stillness of an April wood,
A silver pool, unruffled by the breeze,
The clean expanse of a prairie's solitude,
And calm, unhurried hours—I love these.

I have been tangled in the nets too long;
I shall escape and find my way again
Back to the quiet place where I belong,
Far from the tinseled provinces of men.
These will be waiting after my release:
The sheltered ways, the quiet paths of peace.

For One Who Is Tired

DEAR child, God does not say today, "Be strong."
He knows your strength is spent; He knows
how long
The road has been, how weary you have grown,
For He who walked the earthly roads alone,
Each bogging lowland, and each rugged hill,
Can understand, and so He says, "Be still,
And know that I am God." The hour is late,
And you must rest awhile, and you must wait
Until life's empty reservoirs fill up
As slow rain fills an empty upturned cup.

Hold up your cup, dear child, for God to fill,
He only asks today that you be still.

The Presence

"WHERE two or three are gathered together," Lord,
We have your promise that you will be there;
We cling to it: your dear unbroken word;
We bring the burdens that we cannot bear;
We bring our heart's deep gratitude and praise
And all the supplications of our days.

And you are here among us as we plead;
We reach our hands to touch your garment's hem.
Your treasure house is opened for our need
As much for us today, Lord, as for them
Who walked beside you on the earthly roads,
And found your hand beneath their heavy loads.

So Lord, within our midst, and by our side,
Continue still to be our strength and guide.

It Has Taken Long

IT has taken long for me to learn
 The simple lessons that the Master taught:
 To consider the lilies as their petals burn
Among the wayside grasses, to take no thought
Of a tomorrow that may never bring
Some direful, long anticipated thing;
To mark the sparrows on a windy stem
Lashing and dipping in a day of storm,
And to remember that He cares for them,
And shelters them and keeps them from all harm;
And that I am more valuable than they
To Him who walks beside me day by day.

"Let not your heart be troubled . . . " —these His
 words
Should have been learned and heeded long ago.
I should have lived light-hearted as the birds;
I should have marked the lilies—Ah, too slow
Has been my heart in learning how to live.
Dear God, You tried to teach me. Please forgive.

"If You Are Quiet"

AN old man sat one evening by his door;
His face was tranquil, in his eyes was peace,
His hands were still, his long life work was
    done,
He had a look about him of release.

And I, who needed much to learn the things
That he had learned, sat down beside him there
On the low doorstep in the scented dusk;
He smiled his gentle smile, he touched my hair,
He said: "My child, I, too, was restless once;
I, too, was hurt by life, and blind and dumb
I groped my way; then a wise one said these words:
'If you are quiet, so will help come.'
'Twas an old folk saying from an old loved land.
I listened to its teaching, listened long,
And learned its secret: He who trusts in God,
And who goes quietly, he will grow strong."

Listening

IF I can learn some lesson through this pain,
　　If I can hear God's voice above the storm,
　　And catch His words and pass them on again
To other suffering ones, if I can warm
Some troubled heart with cheer and sympathy,
And help it find a haven of release,
If I can speak the words God speaks to me
To one soul that has lost its poise, its peace,
This, even this, shall not have been in vain!
God keep me quiet, keep me very still,
That through the heavy darkness and the rain,
The thunder crashing loud upon my sill,
I may discern Your voice, that I may hear
The gentle, helpful, loving words You say.
The storm runs high, God make the words quite
　　　　clear,
And I shall listen carefully today.

At the Beautiful Gate

I TOO, have sat at the Beautiful Gate
Of the temple, asking alms,
Begging for paltry copper coins
To be tossed to my out-stretched palms.
Asking for little, receiving less:
A penny, a stone, a curse,
When all the while at my waiting side
Was the wealth of the universe:

The Beautiful Gate that would let me in
To the house of the living God;
The healing touch that would bid me rise
And leap on the earth's bright sod;
The power of prayer upon which to draw
For all of my vital need;
For the garments of praise for my heaviness,
And Bread upon which to feed.

To One In Sorrow

LET me come in where you are weeping, friend,
   And let me take your hand.
I, who have known a sorrow such as yours,
Can understand.
Let me come in—I would be very still
Beside you in your grief;
I would not bid you cease your weeping, friend,
Tears bring relief.
Let me come in—I would only breathe a prayer,
And hold your hand,
For I have known a sorrow such as yours,
And understand.

Strange Alchemy

I AM amazed to find that pain and grief
By some strange alchemy, if bravely borne,
Become a power, vital beyond belief,
To bless and comfort other hearts that mourn.
I did not dream through those far lonely days,
Those bitter hours when pleading for release,
That God would move in His mysterious ways
To make those hours a means to others' peace.

That one's own darkness may become a light
For hurt, bewildered ones—'tis strange to me;
Yet out of pain is often born a white
Undying flame of love and sympathy;
The power that comes to dry another's tears
Was generated through long bitter years.

The Righteous

FRIEND, do you mourn the passing
       Of some loved one today?
       Try to remember that often
"He taketh the righteous away
From the evil to come." He watches
Above us with infinite care,
And He sees that the future may be
Too hard for a heart to bear;
And so in His loving mercy
He signals that one to come
Into the light and the glory
Of an eternal home,
To be safe and sheltered forever.
"He taketh the righteous," He said,
"From the evil to come." O mourner,
May you be comforted.

To a Journeying Comrade

TO you who are bearing a load up some steep
hillside,
        Burdened with grief and sorrow, or pain
and care,
I have a word to say to you, O journeying comrade:
Do not despair.

You never can tell at all at what near turning
Some pleasant vista may meet your tired eyes
To lift your spirit up and dispel your weeping
With glad surprise.

You never can know what lies beyond a hilltop,
Perhaps some shadowy valley, cool and sweet,
Whose gentle downward sloping, after your climb-
ing,
May rest your feet.

Always, O comrade, there is the chance that your
burden
May slip from your back before the wayside dawn,
And O, my comrade, no matter how hard the going,
Keep on. Keep on!

HAND SET IN FOUNDRY GARAMOND TYPE BY
ARTHUR & EDNA RUSHMORE AT THE GOLDEN
HIND PRESS IN MADISON NEW JERSEY
PRINTED AND BOUND
BY THE HADDON CRAFTSMEN
PUBLISHED BY HARPER & BROTHERS OF NEW YORK AND LONDON